WIRED TO BE WOWED

WIRED TO BE WOWED

Great Marketing Isn't an Accident

MATT BAILEY

THRONE
PUBLISHING GROUP

Throne Publishing Group
2329 N Career Ave #215
Sioux Falls, SD 57107

One should use common words
to say uncommon things.

—Arthur Schopenhauer

Contents

1 The Wow Factor — 1

2 Wired to be Wowed — 7

3 Are you Wowing or Being Wowed? — 15

4 Know Who You Are — 29

5 Audience — 41

6 Medium — 57

7 Think Like a Publisher — 75

8 Data, Data, Data — 89

9 One Company – One Plan — 103

About The Author — 107

1 | The Wow Factor

Have you ever wondered what makes customers go wild over some companies, and yet ignore others?

Why can some brands effortlessly draw a raving fan base, while others are just "there?"

How do some companies "just get it," while others keep making one mistake after another?

I've been in digital marketing for over 20 years and have dealt with thousands of businesses. In all of the situations I've encountered, this has been the most fundamental question in my mind, "What is the key factor between the success of the 'haves,' and the failure of the 'have nots?'"

What is the factor that gives some companies consistent momentum and success, and what is the factor that makes others unable to increase revenue, despite multiple marketing campaigns? I asked myself these questions after nearly every engagement and realized that there is a simple answer: a culture of strategic thinking.

Consistently successful companies have a defined, articulated, customer-focused strategy, which utilizes data to support decisions. They invest in the right tactics. They find creative ways to use social media and engage customers at a much deeper level. They are the ones that make many more right decisions than wrong ones, and consequently, they see results. Why? Because they know what to do, why they are doing it, and how to read their data to improve.

Conversely, the companies that want growth without goals constantly search for a social media campaign, search engine rankings, or a new website. Granted, all of these are important things, but their results are inevitably sporadic. They experience better rankings, more followers, and sometimes-increased sales, but usually they experience no dramatic business change. Here is the difference: they cannot articulate WHAT their intended goals are or WHY they have those specific goals. They've never considered long-term strategy beyond the immediate tactic!

Their expressed goal is more sales or more leads, but between the desire and the result lies a gray area. Basic questions of strategy get left open or unanswered. Their self-diagnosis results in trying to find an answer for their immediate problem of sales using the buzzword tactic of the day—things like SEO, Facebook, Twitter, blogs, link development, article writing, etc. But the basic question of strategy is never addressed within that company. It's a problem of thinking that Step One is using Facebook and Step Three is making money. Step Two is an afterthought. Maybe, they think it will materialize during Step One? Or maybe, they've never given thought to Step Two at all.

STRATEGY IS STEP ONE

A number of recent studies point to this systemic problem within company culture. The first study that caught my eye unveiled that the majority of marketers identify a lack of strategy as their main obstacle rather than a lack of budget! Other identified obstacles were a lack of training, knowledge, and clear metrics.

So, in other words, the biggest obstacles that marketers face are *what* to do, *how* to do it, and knowing *why* it's working. Those are serious questions!

Shortly after examining this study, another one came across my desk. It presented that fewer than 30% of companies have an identified customer messaging process. 35% of companies claimed an established message development process but admitted that it isn't followed consistently. Another 30% do not have any formalized messaging process and noted that there was no accountability to follow one even if it existed.

Those are some pretty serious issues; and the heart of it all is a *culture of strategy.*

You will not Wow customers without a strategy. Or maybe you will—just not in the way that you intend…

Keep reading and you will understand more about Wowing your customers the right way and for the right reasons. Thus, *Wired to be Wowed.*

Q: What makes customers and audiences love certain companies and not others?

A: That company is Wired to Wow their customers—who are Wired to be Wowed.

Wired to be WOWED

2 Wired to be Wowed

As humans, we are wired to be amazed at things, people, places, events, and even—dare I say—ourselves. We are wired to be drawn to the new, the cool, the hip, the shrewd, and the secretive.

Consider this: You don't need to worry about how you can Wow your potential customers as much as you need to first be aware that they are, quite literally, *Wired to be Wowed*. They are all going to be Wowed by someone or something in some way this very day. This can be for better or for worse. They can have great experiences and terrible ones. Someone is going to get their attention just as sure as the sun is going to set tonight.

My hope with this book is to help you grow in understanding this principle in order to move beyond the question from *if* you can Wow your customers to *how*, *when*, and *where* you will wow them. You stop hoping to Wow them and simply plan on doing it.

To elaborate further, consider why people go to the Grand Canyon. Why do they love to sit at the US Capital on the 4th of July and watch the fireworks despite the relentless traffic? Why do we travel for an entire day across the country to see a show that lasts one hour? To be Wowed.

We crave to be Wowed. Being Wowed sends us to emotionally heightened spaces within ourselves. We seek that feeling, both in healthy ways and in unhealthy ways. In fact that much of what motivates our behavior is caused by this insatiable desire to be Wowed. We *need* it. We *want* it. Isn't it bizarre how we humans find ways to get the things we want and need regardless of the obstacles? Your customers are going to get Wowed and they won't stop until they are.

As a consumer, being wowed is a passive experience. It happens to us by utilizing what is in us. Getting followed-up with at just the right time, a recommended product based on a past purchase, a quick thank you for adding a product review—these are some of the things that make us feel special, a part of something bigger, and feel like we've been noticed. Something sparks in our brain when we perceive that we have a relationship with a brand or a company they just know us, and the best part is ,we are participating in that relationship!

The interesting thing about being wowed is that it doesn't seem to go deep; rather it evokes an almost immediate response in us. Most of the time, we don't even think about it. We click, we like, we vote, we respond, and we look at a brand's product. We have this wired response that reacts in that Wow moment.

Of course, some brands do it better than others. Some marketing consistently grabs our attention, yet other strategies are easy to ignore. Some emails immediately hit the bin, while others grab our gaze.

What makes this happen? The companies who understand that their customers are Wired make it their mission to Wow in every communication.

Somebody is wowing your customers right now. Why not you?

2

How does understanding how your
customers are Wired To Be Wowed change your
marketing conversation?

What is one way in which you will think differently
as a result of this chapter?

3

Are You WOWING or Being Wowed?

3 Are you Wowing or Being Wowed?

This desire to be Wowed can work for us or against us.

The Wow factor not only exists for your customers, but also for you, the business owner.

The problem in business is that we get distracted by new social media, the latest sales guru, or the next big marketing breakthrough system that we hope will redeem our last ten attempts that failed miserably.

This is a problem. A sickness, really. And now we are going to define it.

SHINY OBJECT SYNDROME

Yes, that's the diagnosis. What are the symptoms?

- A strange attraction to headlines about the latest social media
- Thinking that the latest tactic will increase your business
- Self-diagnosing marketing choices based on articles, hearsay or assumptions
- Lack of internal marketing measurement and data
- A string of past marketing agencies that couldn't do the job
- Stagnation – a lot of activity, but not a lot of results

Ultimately, I've found that Shiny Object Syndrome (SOS) is a mindset that believes the answer is *out there*, and not *in here*. Those suffering from Shiny Object Syndrome are always looking to **external factors** such as new technology, social media tactics, or a new agency.

However, those that are immune to Shiny Object Syndrome are laser-focused on **internal factors**: marketing and website analytics, cross-channel tracking, sales tracking, and customer insights. They know *what's* working, *why* it's working, and *how* to leverage that data into informed decisions.

At the most basic level, a business that suffers from Shiny Object Syndrome is one that is negatively distracted by advances in technology and media. In contrast, a business that is Wired to Wow is one that proactively implements those advances as an extension of existing strategy. We all want to be a part of businesses that Wow, but what does that look like? What are the functional differences within this dichotomy?

In this chapter, I want to demystify the major distinctions between these two kinds of operations and present to you what a business that "Wows" looks like.

THREE SHINY OBJECTS

As a consultant, I've discovered three major Shiny Objects that distract and paralyze business leaders and employees alike: *new technology, the assumptive promise of technology, and emotions.* Understanding each of these will help us avoid distraction and stay on course with the true vision of our companies.

Technology offers to simplify our work and lives. But it does more than just that. To businesses, it offers the prospect of greater profit (more money) and the idea that it will make our work better. Frequently, we hear of businesses making lots of money through technology channels like Twitter. From the outside, it appears so easy. *Well, we could do that too,* we think to ourselves. Unfortunately, when we are Wowed by the technological success of others, we only see the attractive return, but we rarely consider the investment it cost them.

New technology provides an easy answer to why you may not be successful—I call this its **assumptive promise**. Underneath the external lure of technology is the promise that it will fix all your problems. It is something like: *x amount of new customers, x amount of sales in x amount of time.* As tempting as it looks we both know it is unrealistic. The Wow of technology lies in its promise to immediately revamp productivity and bolster the success of our businesses. But, it's a false promise. Yes, new technology is a fundamental tool in marketing today (and one with great potential), but we cannot count on it to fix our business' foundational problems. Usually, the problem is too deep for technology alone to solve.

The last major element of Shiny Object Syndrome is our own **emotions**. When we sense that our businesses are failing in an area— or altogether—we worry as we seek answers. I have consulted with businesses that are deeply convinced they *need* to incorporate a new website into their strategy. They believe the primary reason they are falling behind is that their current website is not up to date or on par with the trends. However, when I ask *why* they believe a new website will fix their problems, they generally lack facts and data to back up the belief. In essence, they are responding out of emotion. I think you and I can agree that a business driven by pure emotion will not thrive for long.

When a business is enamored by the headlines, technology, or trendy conference talks of the day, they are losing grip of the dynamics in their own business. When shiny objects are distracting your team, it means you are looking for answers outside of the data native to your organization. Ironically, that is the very information you need most. Among other havocs, this habit breeds a culture of instability within your business which results in constant turnover, shifting direction, and perpetual confusion. On the other hand, a successful business must grow teams that are Wowed by their own internal information. They are Wired into their data, website analytics, business measurements, and customer feedback. Those are the teams that come up with ideas about how to better serve their customers and how to improve themselves.

The most significant mark of a thriving business is that they value and depend upon their own data. Don't look outside. Look inside.

LEADING TO WOW

I want to spend some time specifically addressing business leaders about these ideas. The leader's role is to provide the direction and wherewithal for his or her followers to complete a job or arrive at a destination. If leaders themselves are distracted by the Shiny Objects constantly presented in the media, they will simply never be capable of guiding their business to success. Especially as one with influence and power, it can be tempting to frequently "field test" new tactics. While it's good for a leader to be aware of trends in the industry, a better leader understands how to use them as a compliment to their strategy. What I mean is this: your data is the most accessible and valuable information you have to increase profits. Looking elsewhere is only helpful to a degree if you haven't looked inside first.

Also, leaders must remember that if they are distracted by shiny objects, their teams will be distracted by them as well. Employees learn quickly that they will be rewarded for finding new shiny objects, if that is the goal. If you are continuously adjusting your company's strategy to accommodate every new and trendy social media channel you will eventually overload your team with too much work. As I have already mentioned, the process of keeping up with technology today is a constant sprint. Weighing down your employees (and yourself) with too many channels or too much external information will only hinder your strategy's momentum. This is evidence that proves a lack of direction. Before you find yourself suffering from Shiny Object Syndrome, decide where you are going and which channels will help get you there.

To help you answer questions like these, I want to offer a three-step-guide which will allow you to filter the plethora of new concepts and influences in your industry. These steps can function as guardrails to keep you on track with your business's strategy and overall objectives.

1. Data & Analytics

You guessed it: the first step is to know your own data. This means knowing what makes you the most money, what particular channels are the most profitable, and why. Being able to analyze your own data and measurements is *the single most important step of the filtering process*. Becoming effective in this area will prove a lens through which you will see every aspect of successful marketing differently. Your own data is the standard. If you have objective data that proves one channel (i.e. your blog) is generating income, you now know it will be counterproductive to take money from your blog and allocate it to another channel. Essentially, if you are not familiar with your own data, you will not have a good basis for making decisions.

2. Ask, "How does this channel fit our culture, message, and personality?"

With the appropriate analytics in place, you are now free to make choices based on their effectiveness to support and extend your strategy. Does this new possibility amplify what you are already doing, or do you have to adjust your strategy to make it work? This is about accommodation. Certain channels may fit your personality and resources as a company, whereas others simply won't suit the company at all. If you have the assets, talent, and resources to incorporate a new channel—great! If not, what resources do you need to attain it? When considering a new business idea, first discern the *return*. Will this monetize? Secondly, measure the investment it demands. What will this cost?

3. Strategy

The objective of utilizing new channels is to enhance and support your strategy. Signing up on Pinterest and posting motivational quotes probably doesn't count. Just *using* a social medium is not a strategy— but how you use that medium can either help or hinder your strategy. Of course, this requires that you understand both strategy and audience. The worth of every tweet, blog post, or email can be gauged by how closely it supports and works within your strategy.

Here is an example of Shiny Object Syndrome and how seductive it is. In the early days, Twitter was the darling of the tech media. Here are a series of headlines about Dell increasing their revenue with Twitter:

December 2008, *Digital Beat*:
"Twitter Has Made Dell $1 Million in Revenue"

June 2009, *Information Week*:
"Dell Makes $3 Million From Twitter-Related Sales"

December 2009, *Mashable*:
"Dell Rides Twitter to $6.5 Million in Sales"

Now, that's not attractive at all, is it? Dell making millions of dollars from using Twitter?

That is one big Shiny Object.

Let's apply our 3-step "filter":

1. Data & Analytics: Let's add some perspective and context to these numbers. One of the most important numbers that jumps out is the "millions of dollars." Who doesn't get excited about that? Well, even more thrilling is doing a quick search to find Dell's annual revenue: around $60 billion! Have you done the math yet? At an average of $3 million/year, that Twitter revenue would only account for less than 0.01% of Dell's annual revenue.

2. How does this fit? Now that we have some context, let's look at how Dell used Twitter. Primarily, they used it as a customer-service mechanism. Dell put a team of customer service technicians on Twitter to respond immediately when someone had a Dell-related issue or question. Dell had the resources available to apply an existing resource to a new medium.

3. Strategy. For Dell, Twitter allowed them to reach their primary audience through an immediate conversation. Dell is a computer brand and their customers are computer users, most of whom are online, and many are early adopters. By gaining traction among the early adopters, they were able to reach one of their target audiences.

Context is everything, isn't it?

I'm not saying that Twitter isn't useful. If that's what you are thinking, then you are thinking tactically, not strategically. The context of
this example is to help us better evaluate how Twitter was used to reach
a specific audience by a specific company and to help you think cre-
atively. Looking for the additional context on how new technologies
are used in these "headlining" case studies enables you to fill in the
gaps between the use and the profitability of a tool.

To avoid getting distracted by Shiny Objects, protect yourself by
evaluating them through these steps. By understanding how other
businesses are utilizing tools and technology, you'll start to see that
success is based on HOW it is used, and not by simply being used.

To conclude, I want to paint a picture of a business that is Wowing—a
business that has the industry's attention because of their impeccable
dedication to *their own success*. I believe the first goal of such a business
is *customer service*. They have defined their customer base and a long-
term customer journey. They are invested in those customers, and they
know the appropriate conversations that need to take place within
those relationships. Further, this business has the data that provides
feedback to root them in the reality of their situation. In other words,
such a business is not so concerned with externals. This is what I call
a data-centric feedback process. Such a process ensures that they are
reaching the right customers with the right message at the right time.

Whether or not such a business exists for you right now, it is an
ideal worth the effort. My hope is that this chapter has provided you
with enough information and motivation to pursue the right changes
in your business—changes that will keep you from distraction. Maybe
your business will be exactly what Wows us next.

1

What percentage of your day are you spending getting Wowed and by what? What about your team?

What are you going to do in order to make sure
you and your team have a clear filter?

2

3

Who are some other sources
you trust that can give you feedback
for your filter and when will you reach out to
them to discuss this?

Know WHO You Are

4 Know Who You Are

Now that you are aware that you and your customers are W2bW and that Shiny Object Syndrome (SOS) is a virus that affects marketing professionals everywhere, how do we begin apply this understanding to our business so we can grow our companies and change our world?

It starts with knowing who you are, knowing your identity or your narrative.

Socrates was on-point when he said, "Know Thyself." If you don't know who you are or what *exactly* your message is, your social media posts will do nothing but confuse your audience. You must have a story or a narrative that clearly depicts who you are.

When you have a successful narrative, every single post and communication will be built around this foundational aspect of your social media campaign. Every post, blog, tweet, and video you make from this point forward will communicate with authentic consistency, and you will build trust.

A prime example of this was a company in the UK called Death Cigarettes. If you ever had the opportunity to buy them, you would have actually read slogans such as, "Let Us Be The Nail In Your Coffin." In one year, this brand of cigarette became a top seller in the UK.

Why? They knew who they were and communicated with authentic consistency. They told the truth in an industry where companies were lying, and Death Cigarettes quickly became the highest selling product.

WHO ARE YOU?

When you have clearly answered this question you are ready for social media, but not a moment before. I would rather be blunt and save you money, as opposed to motivate you to do something you aren't ready to do. Until you know who you are and what your message is, you will not be profitable on social media.

Take the top four insurance agencies, for example:

Progressive: "A Voice of Reason"

State Farm: "A Friend"

Geico: "An Entertainer"

Allstate: "A Fear: What if?"

Think of how much this makes sense as we go through the reasoning for their narratives. Progressive is the voice of reason in the industry. This gives birth to the character "Flo." She shows you their rates and those of their competitors. You are the one who chooses based on all the information they provide.

State Farm always wants to be your friend and neighbor. They are always on your side. They are the anchor in your community that everyone can count on.

Geico is the entertainer. They have the caveman, the gecko, and the pig to name a few.

Allstate employs fear-based selling. They have the character Mr. Mayhem who gets you to think about all the things that could happen to you.

Now, you don't see those exact tag lines in their marketing pieces, but as you stop and think about the nature of their campaigns, it all falls in line with the narratives I have listed above. They're consistent.

Narrative is the statement that defines you. It may not be the exact statement that is your consumer facing slogan or brand, but it is the statement that every single person on your marketing team should be able to repeat verbatim.

Here's the trick. Can you tell me who you are (your business) in less than 3 sentences? Don't give me the elevator pitch; no one has that kind of time or attention any more.

3 sentences? Even that is too long.

How about 1 sentence? And don't use jargon; "Enterprise Application Solutions" doesn't mean anything to me. What do you do?

Now. Make it five words or less.

Here's a hint. Stop using the word "and." In five words, just tell me what you do and define your value to the marketplace. Do you want to Wow new customers? This is where it starts. Get Wired to Wow by creating a short, simple value statement. Do it right, and your market will be Wowed.

1

What are 5 single words that
define your narrative or who you are
to your customers?

What are the 5 single words that describe the
benefits your customers most want from
doing business with you?

2

3

What are the key words
your successful clients use
in describing the benefit they received
from working with you?

What are the single words that best describe
why you are in business?

4

5

How do your answers to the
previous questions help you craft
your narrative?

AUDIENCE

5 Audience

On Sunday afternoons in the fall, I'm watching football. So when I saw this feature on ESPN about football and data, I was hooked. Data, Dallas Cowboys, and an IBM programmer seemed an interesting combination, and I saw an immediate application. (The video can be viewed here: http://espn.go.com/video/clip?id=12037311)

Here's the gist. Shortly after entering the NFL in the early 1960's, the Dallas Cowboys realized they needed help. Being an expansion team, the Cowboys were behind and couldn't keep up with the others. The only way they could improve was through the draft.

After much deliberation on how to improve their draft choices, the Cowboy's made a choice to hire a computer programmer and statistician from India to work for the team. A. Salam Qureishi, an expert data analyst who worked for IBM, was brought to Dallas to develop a computer system that could objectively quantify and rank the skills of football players. This way, the Cowboy's could figure out exactly whom they needed to draft to improve as a team.

Qureishi's first question to the Cowboys changed everything. He asked, "What makes a good football player?"

That statement stuck with me as I watched the documentary. It stuck with me as I reflected that very few companies could answer that question if it were phrased like this: "What makes a good customer?"

You see, we have business goals, professional goals, and even personal goals. But how many businesses have customer goals?

- What is a good customer?
- How would you define or measure that?
- What is the end goal of a customer relationship with our company?

Thinking like this leads to profitable consequences. It leads to even better questions and more thoughts:

- What is the value of a customer?
- What is the value of a good customer?
- What is the lifetime value of a good customer to our business?
- What is our customer turnover rate?
- How do I transform an average customer into a good customer?
- Who are our highly profitable customers?
- Where did they come from?

Ouch! Have you ever asked those questions?

Personally, once I started thinking in those terms, I dramatically grew my business because I had the data to show which of my customers were the best, longest-term, and most profitable. Also, I knew how they came to be clients. Armed with that data, it was a simple decision to change my marketing to focus on the type of customers that were good ones!

Similarly, The Cowboys changed their thinking and had dramatic success in the draft. They found players in other sports. Some had never played football, but they fit the definition of a "good player." In the 60's and 70's, they went on a winning streak that remains unmatched today.

The fundamental requirement of successful marketing is to know the group of customers with whom you hope to make connections. This is called your target audience.

It is extremely difficult and unprofitable to execute marketing and sales when you do not have a good idea *whom* you are trying to target. That is why I propose the first step marketers should take when considering their customer base is to ask this question: *what is a good customer?*

Now, when it comes to marketing, a single definition of the "ideal customer" does not fit every business model. However, every business should take the time to determine what that customer looks like for them. Here are a few questions to help you and your team find the ideal customer:

- How do we define a "good" customer?
- How do we define other types of customers?
- How do we move each type of customer into being a good customer?
- What is the ideal customer journey?
- Who are my good/profitable customers?
- What sources brought them?
- Which sources provide highly profitable customers?
- Which sources provide low profitability customers?
- What are common factors in this analysis?
- What do "good" customers have in common?

When you begin to answer questions like these, your ideal customer will start to emerge. These answers reveal characteristics about customers that will actually help you define what *ideal* means to you.

From here, you can now measure your own customers with that definitive standard. Either your customers meet this ideal (this is usually not the case), or they miss the mark in some way. Perhaps this means you need to adjust your target audience or your marketing strategy. But the first step is always to ask, *what is our ideal customer?*

WHO IS MY CUSTOMER?

Essentially, these questions also show you how much you actually know about your customers. Accordingly, it makes good sense to consider the systems you have in place to learn even *more* about them. For instance, if all you do is process orders and never develop a better understanding or ask for more information about your customers, you have a limited pool of information to develop. With a limited pool of information, you limit the ways you can reach and satisfy them.

Maybe it will be of use to you to send out a customer survey to learn more about their experience with you. I have found that meeting one-on-one with a valued customer is an invaluable way of learning more about their perspective of your interactions with them. If one customer has an objection or recommendation, it is likely that others will too. The more you can learn about your audience, the more effectively you can reach them.

Many businesses that reach out for customer feedback are often surprised at what they find. More times than not, the company feels they are strong in a specific area, only to discover that their customers feel differently. Perhaps they feel you need to improve in customer service, all the while you believed it was your strongest area. No matter what, the customer's thoughts are invaluable because they are the ones you are aiming to reach.

Determining your ideal customer can start with a basic demographic. Who are your most immediate and obvious customers? If you are selling golf aids you will likely be marketing primarily to men between the ages of thirty and seventy. However, the ways you connect with a thirty-year-old are vastly different than the ways you will a seventy-year-old. Simply put: know your audience.

STAY THE COURSE

With a solid understanding of your ideal and present customers, many marketers tend to shift their focus to other businesses that also compete for a similar customer base. I tend to advise against this for one important reason: everyone assumes their competitors are *doing it right*.

Time and time again I have discussions with clients who are completely caught up in how their competitors are marketing. The problem is that you only have access to the externals; there is no way of knowing, from the outside, if your competitors have a clearly defined audience. Further, you do not know if what they are doing is even effectively reaching that audience or is profitable.

While it is good to be familiar with how your competitors are marketing, I believe it is far better to forge your own path. Why? Because the best information you have is the information you generate and the feedback you extract from internal measurements and your own marketing. You do not have real feedback or data from competitors.

We live in a world where everything is personalized. Anything that is generalized will not be heard. The number one reason knowing your target audience is crucial to successful marketing is this: *if you say the same thing to everyone, you're saying nothing to anyone.* If broad and widespread marketing strategies were ever effective, they are no more. We all need to be specific and focused with our messages and means of marketing—and that requires us to know our audience.

YOUR STORY AND THEIR STORY

Asking these questions is what enabled me to see the clear difference between why some companies are successful and some rarely see success. Those that knew their story and their customers' stories were able to connect with an audience that was Wired to be Wowed.

Then, there were those companies that attempted one tactic after another, hoping to see success. What was interesting is that there would often be what I would call secondary success: increases in subscribers, more fans, and even some good engagement. But it was fleeting and temporary. It never translated into business success.

It was a successful tactic, but the company was not able to make it fit within the larger scheme and make it a primary factor in revenue or profitability. The company had success in increasing external factors but was not able to maintain the customer connection enough to drive an internal result. The customer wasn't wowed enough to maintain the engagement.

To keep our customers wowed past the "like" means that we need to know our customers' stories on a personal level. What is driving them to solve their problems with our products? What inspirations cause them to seek out this information? What are they trying to add to their life? Answering these questions brings us into closer contact with our customers' goals and motivations. Marketing is all about understanding their stories and then connecting with them.

Goals and motivations tell us a lot about the stories of our customers. However, goals and motivations are not the same. Shopping with my teenage daughter made this very clear to me. My daughter's goal is to buy shoes and her motivation is to buy shoes that her friends will love. Primarily, she's not seeking shoes for herself. Like most middle school students, she is seeking shoes as a social statement and something her friends will like as well. Her motivations drive her to achieve her goal. In the same way, understanding *both* the goals and motivations of our customers will enable us to connect with them on deeper, more effective levels. And only then can you know how to solve their problems.

Learning a customer's story can be as simple as retracing your past interactions. Read through emails, letters, conversations, or surveys and look for these key points:

- What was their problem?
- How did you solve it?
- Why did they choose you?
- What other factors influenced their decision?
- What additional information did they provide as to their motivation?
- What keeps them as a customer?
- How have they progressed and grown with you?

At this point, you are beginning to learn *why* you were able to connect with your customer and what exactly you did well in that interaction. Customers who feel that you helped them solve a problem are nearly always willing to include information on how exactly you helped. For instance, perhaps a customer will tell you how glad they are with their purchase of your dietary product because; "I've just been struggling to get enough vitamins for months now!" Now, you are learning both your customer's story *and* finding your ideal customers. Knowing precisely what they loved about working with you is just the information you need to continue meeting their needs. Which, of course, tells you so much about how to market to your audience.

On the other hand, retrieving customer interactions from the past will likely reveal those instances when you were *unable* to meet their needs. They had a problem; they sought your product or information, but left with that problem unsolved. While these interactions might be more painful to review, they are equally as important to understanding your audience. If you can see where you went wrong in the past, you can avoid repeating the mistakes in the future. Also, this process will reveal aspects of your customers' stories that are valuable to making connections with them. Don't be afraid to go back and learn from your mistakes. Talk to your customers and learn what they really want and what they don't. Learn their stories.

With one of my past customers, I discovered that price was the number one objection. But, through interviews, we learned that though the price was high, the result was worth it. When people saw results, suddenly the price didn't seem outrageous. As a result, we changed our marketing to be results-oriented. Yes, the price is high, but the end product—the result—is worth it. By adding more result-oriented information from customer features, interviews, and spotlights, my company was able to change the conversation from price sensitivity to quality. My company had the data to adjust the message and turn the primary objection into a primary selling point. This profitable adjustment was only possible because we knew our audience.

Remember, if you say the same thing to everyone, you're saying nothing to anyone. I hope this chapter clarifies the importance of knowing your customer base on deeper levels. Not only do you need to know their available budget, but also their goals, motivations, and stories too. Just like the Cowboys football team was able to thrive once they defined their ideal athlete, I am confident you will be a more effective marketer when you can define your ideal customer.

1

What is the profile of your best
current customers?

What was their story when you
first met them?

2

3

How did their story
intersect with yours?

5

How do you think your customers would
describe your value?

What can we learn from past clients who's
problems were not solved?

6

6 Medium

You have your message, now let's bring it to the world. How you tell your message is through a *medium*—often times referred to as a *channel*. We will discuss the definition of medium as well as its function and to marketing success. Lastly, we will show how the mediums are misunderstood. Why? Because *how* you say something is just as significant as *what* you have to say.

First, let's begin with a proper definition of medium in the world of marketing.

Most simply, *a medium is a singular mode of communication.* This includes everything from email, TV, and direct mail, to Twitter, blogs, and many, many more. As you read this book, you are engaging with the medium by which I have chosen to communicate with you—a book! Sounds pretty simple, right? It is.

The primary reason I've chosen to include a chapter on medium in this book is because every medium carries a different method for communicating information. This means we are all constantly interpreting what is being communicated to us based on what medium that message is using. This fact is so significant that the mantra, developed by Marshall McLuhan, states, "The Medium Is the Message." Think of it this way: if you were to watch an advertisement on television, there is a specific (and limited) amount of information that you will receive. However, the way you interpret that information is due, in part, to the medium of the information—TV. If you were to receive a letter in the mail with the same exact information, you would interpret it quite differently. This is all because a medium's message is received and evaluated in relation to it.

Each particular medium has strengths and weaknesses—so the goal of every marketer should be to find out which ones work best for both their message and audience. We all know that the purpose of our messages is for them to be received and interpreted as we hope, but I don't believe we give that conviction as much consideration as it deserves. How often do you evaluate whether or not your messages are being heard? And heard by the people you want to hear it! This chapter is aimed at helping you discover what medium(s) works best for you and your business, so let's take a look at some of the most important channels in the market today.

1. BLOG

Because content is at the core of successful marketing, I find blogs to be one of the most effective ways to communicate with your audience. A primary reason for this is ownership rights: I own the website, I own the blog, I own the content I produce, I own the works, pictures, videos...I own it all! This makes for simplified analytics and allows me to track and see what customers are doing on my site. On the other hand, blogs demand a *lot* of content. If your audience is going to pay attention to your blog, you need to produce new and interesting content at a very rapid rate. If not, people will simply stop visiting the site.

People can find what they want on Google in a split second. If we don't keep our content up-to-date, we will be lost and left behind in the flurry of information. Today, marketers have become publishers—constantly thinking ahead, constantly producing new content. So, we see that while blogs are favorable for their ownership rights, that pro is counterbalanced by the constant demand for fresh content and consistent management.

If you are *creating* the content for your blog, I recommend you invest at least ten to fifteen hours a week developing new material. If you are *curating* content for your blog, I recommend between five and ten hours of analyzing data and visitor tendencies. This is more than just sitting down and hammering out article after article. Anyone can do that. Rather, the kind of blog content that *works* is nuanced and interesting. Take time to say what you want to say, but also take time to ensure that the *way* you are saying it is creative.

Financially speaking, blogs and web sites can cost anywhere from a few hundred to a few thousand dollars to develop—depending on how much of the work you do yourself. In the end, blogs and web sites are not huge financial investments, but demand more time than some other mediums, making them one of the biggest long-term investments a company can make. Content marketing has shown itself to be an exceedingly effective way to build an audience, build leads, and—over the long-term—produce the *highest quality* of leads. The payoff is this: the longest-lasting results with the highest-quality customers over the longest term possible.

Content marketing through blogs and web sites is the biggest investment, but it really does have a proportional payoff.

2. EMAIL

The second medium we will cover is Email—one of the most foundational and overlooked elements of communication. Simply put, most people actually *want* to receive their marketing through email, which is a reason it's so widely used today.

If you talk to any marketing professional about email they will all have one piece of advice for you: get that name! As soon as someone gives you their name and email address, they are giving you explicit permission to market to them. This makes email a very personal and direct medium. A list of email addresses is a list of customers, and through your marketing, you can build a relationship with those customers. Let's take a closer a look at the pros and cons of email.

Email is the lowest cost medium, yet it yields a very high pay off. The Direct Marketing Association estimates a $43 return for every $1 invested in email. It is incredibly scalable—meaning you can strategically segment and categorize the recipients of every email you send to ensure the message will be received well. However, it takes planning! Sending a "blast" email every month to ten thousand people isn't going to be effective; but sending a specific message to a particular group of people who have something in common or have shown interest in what you have to offer—that *will* be effective.

Perhaps, the greatest pro and con of this medium is the work it demands. You have to work with it to make it grow, and its effectiveness is based on the work behind the scenes. You must compile categorized lists and set automated actions in place to ensure the right segments of your audience are receiving the right parts of your message. As you scale your audience up, your communications will take even more planning.

The initial planning behind email marketing requires at least *a dozen hours* a week. I'm not talking about the monthly blast email; I'm talking about developing a starter of 2-3 campaigns based on different segments of visitors or customers. Developing lead generation scenarios and lead nurturing campaigns requires planning, mapping and developing a story through your emails.

However, once those plans and actions are set in place with some sort of system—such as automated emails—your investment will reduce. Financially, email is the lowest cost medium available (it starts free!). When I evaluate businesses, email is consistently the lowest investment medium with the highest return. While, on the other hand, blogs and web sites are high investment, high return mediums. Yet again, we see the huge importance of knowing what mediums are most appropriate for our messages.

3. VIDEO

Video marketing is being used in many creative ways today. I like to refer to it as the salt of online marketing because of the way it's "sprinkled" over other marketing systems to add flavor, appeal, and charisma. Videos can be easily integrated into so many other mediums with a short link or code, making them quite portable. However, they have truly become a medium of their own in recent years (e.g. video blogs).

Like every medium, videos must contain interesting content. A video blog won't be very effective if your messages and content are boring. You *must* produce content that people want to ingest. That being said, we live in a world where internet users love to watch videos for their information. Most mediums are primarily word based. Video, on the other hand, can carry words, image, emotion, and other nonverbal forms of communication. Often times, this gives video marketing the upper hand with other mediums. Videos don't just tell they show.

The biggest cons of video are cost investment and preparation. Producing a high quality, clean-cut video takes planning on numerous levels—and planning takes time. However, video production is especially dependent upon the audience you're trying to reach. If you are planning to appeal to an audience of young teens, perhaps the video doesn't need to look nice, but you will need to meet their expectations in other areas of content (humor, for example). In this instance, the production investments will be much less. It's all about audience.

4. SOCIAL NETWORKING

Social networking can be broken down into a number of mediums. I will cover the most prominent ones we see today.

Beyond a doubt, Facebook is today's most widely used social network. It is a platform for casual, friendly and, well...*social conversation*. LinkedIn is Facebook's professional counter balance—a platform for business-oriented conversation. While Facebook has the masses, LinkedIn has the attention of the professional community and the highest affluence of any audience. Many business leaders prefer LinkedIn to exchange ideas and find new talent for their companies.

Twitter is another popular social network. It is an *in the moment, stream of consciousness* medium—and is extremely effective for news and networking. What sets Twitter apart from other mediums is the real-time conversation. It processes and emits near endless amounts of information that is here one minute and gone the next. Twitter is constantly demanding that you keep up. If you're not on Twitter, you're missing what's in the *now*. If you're in a business that seeks to communicate in-the-moment information, Twitter is a medium for you.

The down side of this medium is that some businesses simply do not function this way, and the fast-paced character of Twitter simply does not appeal to their marketing strategies. Twitter will not be effective for businesses like these, and *that's okay.*

The last category of social networking mediums is what I call *image-based* sharing. The two most prevalent uses of this type are found in Instagram, Pinterest, and Snapchat today. They are focused around an image that can be anything from a selfie to a recipe. I know one woman who built a successful fashion business on the sole strength of Instagram. By frequently posting pictures of her products and attracting followers from the right audience, she was able to sell her garments at a rapid rate, using the Instagram app as her primary medium of communication. Clearly, this type of marketing will not fit every business model, but this example plainly shows just how diverse the work of marketing mediums is today.

Content is the common core that lies at the center of each of these mediums. If you're developing a marketing team or strategy, I strongly advise you to compile nine months of content (or, at the very least, content ideas) before you start any marketing at all. If you do not, you will be living at the mercy of each one of these mediums—you will never be ahead or proactive. In conclusion, here are a few steps that will help you begin to create a marketing strategy that keenly uses mediums the right way.

Why? Because how you say something is just as significant as what you have to say.

And that gets to the problem that businesses have with marketing through mediums. I have seen countless strategies start with the dangerous combination of enthusiasm and ignorance, only to fail a few weeks into the campaign.

You see, adding a few posts on a blog is not blogging, nor is it marketing. Making a few updates on your company Facebook page is not a strategy. Tweeting 4 updates a day is not a strategy. It is simply using the medium.

The reason so many social marketing campaigns fail is one word:

strategy. They don't know what the end goal looks like. Companies assume that more followers will translate into more revenue but forget to fill in the blank between the campaign and the result.

I have found that when approaching the selection of mediums, the question is not so much "which do I use?" But, more to the point, "What type of conversation do I want to have?"

You see, by changing the question, it changes how you approach each medium. It better equips you to use mediums appropriate to your strengths, resources, time and (most importantly) purpose.

If I want to have an **acquisition conversation** to gain new customers, then your approach will naturally be different. Here are the questions that should arise:

- What mediums would be appropriate to reach out to new customers?
- Where would we find the most appropriate audience for our acquisition message?
- What would those conversations look like?
- How do we expect the audience to respond to that message?
- What is the outcome of an acquisition conversation?
- What are ways to measure that outcome?

If I want to have a **customer engagement conversation**, the questions again become more specific:

- Where are my customers?
- How do I reach them?
- How do I persuade them to engage?
- What do I want them to do?
- How do they engage now?
- What do we expect from the engagement?
- What is the outcome of an engagement conversation?
- What are ways to measure that outcome?

You'll notice that the final questions of each sample conversation focus on expectations and measurements. These are the critical elements of any conversation or campaign. How will you know that your conversation was effective if you do not first develop a method of tracking the involvement or completion?

Instead of looking at marketing mediums as individual parts, especially in the case of social media, look at it as an engine. Each function affects the next function. Rather than using Instagram because it's Instagram, ask yourself if Instagram fits into your intended conversation with your target audience.

A great example of this was sent out by United Airlines. I use this example in all of my talks because it shows how a large organization utilized their strengths and developed conversations that naturally fit the medium.

For instant answers to questions, Twitter is the ideal medium. For behind-the scenes access to hangars, cockpits and flight control, YouTube works well. For vacation photos, Instagram is key. If you are interested in careers, LinkedIn is effective.

What I love about the following example is that United is telling the customer, "depending upon your need, here is the best way to have a conversation with us." Despite all the mediums, this fantastic message was sent out to existing customers through email…

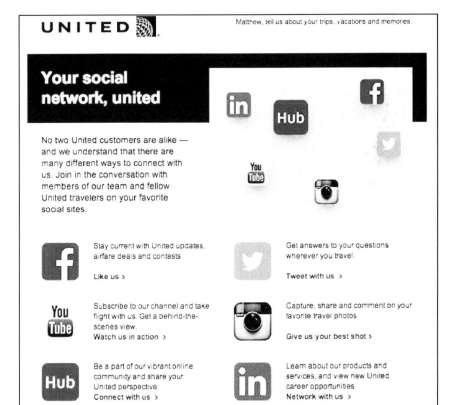

1

Where are our customers
on social media? Are they even
on social media? If so, will they be open
to marketing?

What are they doing on social media? Posting pictures? Sharing articles? Learning from groups?

2

3

What are the mediums we
are using and how effective are
they today?

4

5

What kind of conversations are we currently having? Are they being measured?

7 Think Like a Publisher

One of the best ways to understand effective marketing is to look at the work of a publisher. If you subscribe to any catalogue or magazine, you might notice how new monthly editions are released long before the month is even here. Many magazines begin to promote Christmas content just after school starts in the fall. Why is this? Publishers plan ahead. They don't wait for trends to manifest themselves. Publishers know that the trend is coming and initiate the conversation about what's just around the corner. They know what's coming, and that's showcased in what they publish.

Too often I see retailers simply miss their opportunity to market in advance by waiting until the last minute. Digital retailers that wait until the fall to figure out their December sales strategy are already behind the curve. To market like a publisher means you must see the oncoming trends and capitalize on them far in advance. This kind of marketing demands a particular mental framework. Here are three fundamental features of a publisher mindset:

1. IDENTIFY THE TREND
Obviously, the only way to market ahead of the game is to actually know

the upcoming trends. But while knowing the trends means thinking ahead, that doesn't always mean you know them. This is not a guessing game so much as it is an analysis of your past and current marketing strategies. I am amazed at how many people don't look back to their past performance throughout the year to guide them forward. A good analytics and CRM (Customer Relationship Management) setup can help you identify the focal points of traffic spikes in the past. Also, basic search engine keyword research tools are a great help in discovering trending words and phrases that relate to your industry. Such procedures will assist you in identifying oncoming trends. Often, thinking ahead starts with thinking back.

2. UNDERSTAND THE TREND

A list of questions gives way after you identify a trend: Why does this trend take place? Who is it that's looking for this information? Are they pre-planners or last-minute people? How can I engage with this trend and these people? Obviously, identifying a trend is of little use if you are unable to step into conversation with it and encounter it. By answering questions like these, you can begin to engage with the trend and with the people you want to reach.

3. DEVELOP A STRATEGY

Once you feel you have both identified and grasped the facets of a trend, you must develop a strategy to actually *get ahead of it*. Again, this process begins with a fresh list of questions: How are we going to do this? By what means and medium(s) will we move forward?

One of my clients uses blogging as their primary customer acquisition strategy. Search Engines drive nearly 80% of their new business. Because of this strategy my client must consider both the content and the timeframe in which they hope to publish their articles to even get them into search engines to be seen *at* the trend. This means uploading blog posts at least *two months* before the trend hits which means planning the content of those articles long before they are published.

Not only do you need to know the trend is coming you also need to be months ahead of the *beginning* of the trend to fully implement your marketing strategy in time. This means thinking even further ahead, more planning.

In the case of this client, they have 5 major content trends that drive business throughout the year. Those trends are scheduled on a calendar at least 12-18 months in advance, and then content is planned for each trend. Sometimes, it is a series of articles, interviews or just general information. By planning this far out in advance, there can be strict deadlines imposed moving forward. Planning the content, researching it, and supporting it (with video, infographics or other offers) allows for a strategic assessment of each article, and how it will be promoted once published to the blog. Typically, each blog article is promoted with three to four posts/updates that will be used on the social networks to drive people back to the article (in this case, Facebook is the primary social network). Each update not only links back to the main article but is also designed to spark conversations on that network.

- Plan your articles (What people want to talk about and when!)
- Plan how you will promote your articles through social media or other tactics.
- Plan how you will measure the effectiveness of each article, each medium, and your total strategy.
- Assess how you can improve based on your goals

Interestingly, businesses that have been doing this long-term find that older articles tend to perform the best in driving new visitors. Over time, they gain rankings and increased visibility in search engines. Thus, my client has a curation strategy in place to utilize past articles as acquisition sources throughout the year. Remember, you can't ignore older content – it may be working the hardest!

Releasing an article is the beginning of its life, not the end.

In my experience, the most efficient way to develop a strategy and assure its implementation is to create a long-range content schedule. Simply put, a content schedule is your marketing strategy planned out on a calendar. I believe that the calendar is the most underused tool available to marketers today. It forces you to see your marketing in terms of its sum total, yet allow you to plan precisely and consistently. This plan of attack is much stronger than the, "I need to use Facebook for an hour a day to promote my business" mentality. Rather than mere reaction, it promotes the execution of your plans throughout the entire year.

A good content schedule prompts more helpful questions:

- What is my overall message and how am I developing it?
- When am I going to release this information?
- What does my demographic tell me about when I should release it?
- What time of day is most effective for posting updates?
- What day of the week do I get the most feedback?
- How am I going to promote this article?

When creating an effective content schedule, follow these three steps:

1. MAKE AN HONEST ASSESSMENT OF YOUR RESOURCES

After an article goes live, its success is largely dependent on how well you support it. How you support and spread an article is based entirely on your resources. If part of your content schedule includes promotion via YouTube, you must ensure that you have sufficient assets and funds to cover filming, editing, etc. Or, perhaps you plan to gain a certain number of active followers on Twitter; this requires a good deal of *time*, one of the most important resources. Will you invest time to utilize Facebook as a conversational channel? Does your audience seek this instant interaction? In the end, you must determine what resources you have   and how you can cultivate them to reach your audience effectively.

2. FOCUS ON YOUR PRIMARY CHANNEL

Choose one primary channel with which you will market most frequently and use all other mediums to lead customers towards that channel. If you attempt to use all forms of social media equally, you might find that none of them are considerably helping you gain new readers or buyers. Let one channel be primary, and lead people only to it. Never lead customers to your secondary channels. In my experience, leading customers to secondary sites (like Facebook) as a destination only increases their chances of getting distracted by something other than a link to your article. Focus on your primary channel.

3. MEASURE THE EFFECTIVENESS

The final step is common sense: make sure it's all working. Many marketers struggle due to a lack of strategy rather than a lack of budget. It is vital that you know what you're doing, whom you're reaching, and, especially, how to measure success. Part of your content schedule strategy must include the measurement indicators that will let you know if you're doing the right thing—if it's working.

If your strategy is to drive customers back to your primary channel, a good way to gage success is to measure the *value* of each customer visit. How many customers have visited this article? Often times it is helpful to ask the simple question: am I making money?

Value translates into effectiveness. Always begin by measuring the value of your primary channel. If it lacks value, it lacks effectiveness.

To market ahead of the trend means to think like a publisher.

1

How does thinking as a publisher change my
approach to our marketing plans?

On a scale of 1-10, how would we rate our
content if we were the consumer?

2

3

What does it mean that publishing
an article is the beginning of its life?
How are you supporting publishing or posting
efforts for long-term effect?

What measurements are in place to assess the
quality of our efforts? Are we measuring
the intended outcomes?

4

5

**Are our social media efforts based
on strategic planning, or just a felt need
to "update?"**

DATA, DATA, DATA

8 Data, Data, Data

In the previous chapter we discussed how thinking like a publisher is an effective—and even necessary—means to market well. If we are going to get ahead of the trends, we must think ahead of them. In this chapter I would like to focus on the actual execution and success of your content schedule. To do this, we will take a brief but close look at the vitality of data.

Data is the most effective weapon against Shiny Object Syndrome. Only with a focus on data will we move past ineffective and useless tactics to find platforms and strategies that actually reach our audience.

When you know *what* works and *why*, you are less inclined to move money and time from mediums that you know are delivering profitability to something that's unproven or untested.

MEASURING THE WOW

Most companies are satisfied by measuring the easy things like: page views, visits, time on site, social shares, friends, and followers. These are easy measurements because they lack context or deep thought. They are easy numbers to acquire because they have *no direct influence* on your revenue and commonly make results look much better than they actually are.

The more difficult things to measure are the amount of leads you receive from your marketing, the amount of new subscribers, the amount of leads that became customers, and the number of those customers that have become *good* customers. These things are more difficult to measure, as they require work, consideration, and planning. However, these numbers have a direct influence on your revenue.

The first step to obtaining useful data is to break down your analysis into observable layers. Simultaneously attempting to interpret all your data from all your mediums won't help you much. Measure more specifically and you will unearth helpful information. As we have discussed, it is most logical to begin with your primary medium when analyzing marketing success. If your primary medium is a blog, website, or app, it will give you the most data and the most actionable information.

If your aim is to drive customers to your primary medium and that channel is your blog, what data should you expect from it? What exactly should you look for?

THE 3-STEP FORMULA TO TRANSFORM YOUR ANALYTICS

Here is a very simple three-step formula that I believe will transform your analytics. Ask yourself these three questions:

1. What do they want?

If you can determine what your visitors want, you will be better equipped to reach them. For example, you can look for any data that indicate a visitor's *intent* for being on your blog, website, or app. Also, you can track search terms (which signify trends) or ways by which visitors come across your page, which indicates something about what they want. You can ask more questions: Did they follow a link to your blog? In what context was that particular link which led them to follow it? An email campaign? A website advertisement? Which Facebook post prompted them to visit your site? Ultimately, learning more about what the visitor wants provides an easy method to start segmenting your visitors based on intent or need.

2. What did they see?

After choosing to go to your website, what is the first thing visitors saw? Did the first page meet their expectations? Did it answer their question? Poor page design or content inhibits people from finding their answer. First impressions are massively important. Making the connection between these first two questions, we need to ask ourselves if visitors are seeing what they want to see and whether or not we're meeting their expectations?

3. What did they do?

If they saw what they wanted, what action followed? Did they make a comment on your blog? Did they purchase your product? Did they sign-up for a free trial or offer? Extracting this data is absolutely vital for placing value on mediums. Either they got what they wanted and left immediately, or they did *not* get what they wanted and left immediately. Regardless, you want to know. Perhaps they watched a video on your site, or maybe they read the first paragraph and left. Whatever the case might be, this is the kind of necessary data you can use to value your mediums and your overall marketing campaigns. And this is precisely what I mean when I say data allows you to streamline your resources with *precision* and *confidence*. You will know what people want, what they saw, and if you were able to provide the answer. Are you happy with that answer?

The key in following this three-step process is that it contextualizes to a visit. If visitors came to one of your articles from a link, where was that link? How is it presented? Is it relevant, and how do those visitors react when they land on the linked page? Does it represent more business? Are people registering, contacting, or purchasing? Or, are they simply leaving after a few seconds?

Asking these three questions to create a single, segmented group enables you to view your marketing efforts through the eyes of small groups of similar visitors who have something unique in common. Without this filter, people tend to view their audience as a homogenous crowd.

The more visitors who attain what they want from your site—regardless of what that is—the more valuable your site is. This is deeper than mere page visit data. It is data that reveals the true value—or failures—of your medium by tracking your audience's actions. To the extent that you can discover how satisfied or dissatisfied your visitors currently are with you blog, site, etc., you can adjust your marketing strategies to keep them coming back, and, thus, increase your profit.

Compared to the other campaigning strategies in the current marketing industry, I believe this analytic portion stands out. There are many who talk about the importance of analytics, but they don't go beyond or beneath their big numbers. No one seems to focus on the true value of data and visitors. Ironically, this is really what gives data its worth. For instance, observing an increase of visitors from last month to this month is great, but it will not catalyze your marketing if you don't know what *kind* of visitors, their context, and the additional value generated from your interaction with them. This is as close as you can come as a marketer to actually knowing your customer base on a personal basis, and the more you know your customer base, the better your chances are of connecting with them in a valuable way.

Big numbers don't help anything. Looking at small, contextual groups of numbers helps you understand which areas you need to refine. Big numbers will lie, but small numbers, in context, tell you a story of what you can do to improve.

After looking at visitor segments and their behaviors, it is healthy to look at your overall efforts in comparison to each other. I've talked about looking at how different mediums are more effective than others, so it's time for you to figure out which media channels are working for you!

In the example on the next page, a retailer has viewed their quarter-ly efforts in a medium comparison. The first major number is looking at total revenue generated by each channel. This is the first look at comparative data. In this case, organic search marketing is the primary revenue generator.

The next important comparison is the visitor value per medium. This is a simple calculation dividing the total channel revenue by the amount of visitors. This gives you the average value of a visitor utilizing that channel. Despite the high numbers of search visitors, the sizable revenue makes search visitors one of the most profitable value visitors. This tells me that organic search marketing is an effective medium and warrants continued investment.

Medium	Visitors	Transactions	Revenue	Conversion rate	Average Value	Per Visit Value	Marketing Cost	Profit	Profit per $
Organic	150,000	3,000	**$200,000**	2.0%	$66	**$1.30**	$15,000	**20%**	**$13.33**
CPC	65,000	1105	**$55,000**	1.7%	$50	**$0.84**	$30,000	**6%**	**$1.83**
Social Assist	45,000	180	**$18,000**	0.4%	$100	**$0.40**	$10,000	**2%**	**$1.80**
Email	55,000	880	**$60,000**	1.6%	$75	**$1.09**	$3,000	**14%**	**$20.00**
Direct	45,000	585	**$40,000**	1.3%	$70	**$0.88**	-	**9%**	
Display	35,000	420	**$20,000**	0.6%	$45	**$0.57**	$6,000	**3%**	**$3.30**
Shopping	10,000	250	**$25,000**	2.3%	$100	**$2.50**	$5,000	**5%**	**$5.00**

Then, after figuring in the marketing budget for each medium, you can derive the profit percentage. I find it more effective to look at the ROI per $1 invested. In this example, organic search marketing provides $13 of profit for every $1 invested. Interestingly, Email provides $20 of profit for every $1 invested. Remember that The Direct Marketing Association found that most businesses average $44 for every $1 spent in email? That means that there is opportunity in the email medium!

Measurements like these help you to align your priorities and find the most effective means for **profitable** marketing. I have seen too many businesses take funds from a profitable medium and use those funds to test new mediums. The risk rarely, if ever, works. By hindering an already profitable medium you rob from your business in two ways: reducing what works and stifling profitability. Utilizing those funds for unproven strategies damages you inversely.

Look at it this way, are you willing to risk taking $5,000 of marketing expense from a medium that produces an ROI of $13 per $1 invested? Are you willing to put those same funds into a medium that may only return $0.80 for $1? That decision could be the potential swing of more than $60,000 of lost profit!

In conclusion, we see that data exhibits the value of your mediums—it shows you what works and why. This is not an argument against social media. It is an argument against ignorance. Simply, there is no substitute for a keen data analysis in your annual content schedule. Such analysis can seem tiresome and overly specific but it is the necessary and preemptive work that must be done before you can get ahead of the trend. So, don't settle for those big numbers, get underneath them and look for threads of trend which will keep you from getting distracted by useless mediums and pave a path to more successful marketing.

1

2

Do I measure the effectiveness
of each medium?

How does measuring using the three-step formula: What do they want?, What did they see?, What did they do? differ from my existing reports. What can I learn from knowing this information?

3

4

How would measuring different
segments and intentions change my
reporting and strategy?

How would knowing my per $1 ROI or Profit per $1
spent change my marketing?

5

ONE COMPANY
ONE PLAN

9 One Company – One Plan

Customers are Wired to be Wowed from clear, concise, and consistent messaging that reaches them through every step of their journey and experience with your brand/company. That type of Wow only comes through careful planning and consideration of each step they take. What is left unplanned by many companies is the customer's "next step" and their intended destination.

As Zig Ziglar once said, "If you aim at nothing, you will hit it every time." To Wow your customers, the journey has to be planned, it must be intentional, and your aim must be nothing less than to truly Wow. A reading through this book your new standard is to Wow the audience that is Wired to be Wowed—plain and simple.

Throughout this book, you have identified the key elements of your strategy to Wow your customers. You have determined:

Your Identity: **Who** are you and what do you bring to the market?

Your Customer: **Who** is your audience and what do they want?

Your Conversation: **What** does your audience talk about and where are they talking?

Your Message: **What** value do you communicate with clarity and consistency?

Your Medium: **Which** medium(s) should you use, and how will the medium(s) influence your audience?

Your Wow: **How** will you do it, and how will you measure your results?

Your Plan: **Where** are you going, how will you get there, and how will you know when you arrive?

ONE STEP FURTHER

I want to ask you to consider some of the biggest questions that we ask in business:

Where are we going?
   And…
How are we going to get there?
In other words…**What's the plan?**

What's your marketing plan? As leaders in marketing and in business, we need to be able to answer these questions with clarity, boldness, and confidence.

You don't need to have every detail ironed out, but you do need to answer these questions without blinking.

One of my goals with this book is not only to get you thinking about marketing and Wowing your Wired customers but also to inspire people to follow you. In other words, I want to help you become a better leader. One aspect of being a great leader is to know where you are going, how you will get there, and why you want to go there in the first place.

No matter how much or how little change is required in your organization, it all starts with YOU. The time is now to step up to the plate and be an agent of change, or as I like to call you, an Agent of Wow. An Agent of Wow doesn't need the title or the position to Wow. They start exactly where they are, they do what they can, and put all of their energy into every action they take.

After all, people are going to buy you before they ever buy your company, product, or service.

ONE COMPANY – ONE PLAN – ONE PAGE.

Here are some very simple questions that, while being short, require a lot of thought, and I implore you to think about these and even contact me to help you think them through:

Where are we going?

What is our definition of success as a company?

How will we know when we are successful?

How will we measure our success?

Ask questions, fill up white boards, eliminate anything that is not essential, and be bold. This will require courage. You can do it. Go forth and Wow yourself, your team, and your customers one experience at a time!

About The Author

Matt Bailey resides in the heart of Hall of Fame City (also known as Canton, Ohio). Aiming to carry on his city's legacy, he is a Best-Selling Author, Marketing Expert, Trainer, and Speaker. Matt is the Digital Marketing Instructor for the Direct Marketing Association in NYC, a member of the Digital Marketing Faculty for Market Motive, and an Online Marketing Certification Instructor.

In February 2006, Matt founded and was the President of SiteLogic Marketing (an e-marketing agency focused on action from data) until he sold it in 2014. He now focuses on education through his speaking and writing. His marketing finesse spans well over two decades and his key know-hows lie in Digital Marketing Strategies, Marketing Analytics, Search Engine Optimization (SEO), Web Site Usability, Content Marketing, Making People Laugh, and many more.

Matt's aim to fame doesn't stop there… he has worked with a vast and wide-ly-known clientele, including Google, ESPN, IBM, Gerber Life, Johnson&Johnson, American Medical Association, Travel Weekly, Apple Vacations, Disney, American Greetings, Proctor & Gamble, Toys R' Us, and countless more. He keynotes conferences around the world, speaking at more than 30 engagements a year, in addition to providing in-house training for companies.

Matt is the author of the must-read book entitled, Internet Marketing: An Hour a Day which focuses on a recognized and simple task-based approach to developing enticing internet marketing campaigns. This gem in book form helps businesses keep the $$$ rolling in and their customer engagement at an all-time high. Ultimately, Matt's wit is especially evident when he takes the over-ly complex aspects of marketing and shrinks them into easy-to-digest tidbits. Even the most non-internet savvy folks can grasp marketing gibberish when Matt guides them.

When he isn't immersed in the universe of marketing and technology, Matt spends most of his time being a husband, a dad (to four girls) and whatever time is left is spent reading history, culture, or philosophy books. As a self-proclaimed coffee snob, he absolutely loves a good cup of Joe—especially while reading.

To find out much more about Matt, visit www.sitelogic.com.